180 ESSENTIAL
VOCABULARY WORDS
FOR 3RD GRADE

Independent Learning Packets That Help
Students Learn the Most Important Words
They Need to Succeed in School

Linda Ward Beech

NEW YORK • TORONTO • LONDON • AUCKLAND • SYDNEY
MEXICO CITY • NEW DELHI • HONG KONG • BUENOS AIRES

Teaching *Resources*

Editor: Mela Ottaiano
Cover design: Brian LaRossa
Interior design: Melinda Belter
Interior illustrations: Mike Moran

ISBN-13: 978-0-439-89734-1
ISBN-10: 0-439-89734-3

2 3 4 5 6 7 8 9 10   31   15 14 13 12 11

TABLE OF CONTENTS

Introduction

Academic vocabulary refers to words that are commonly found in textbooks and used in assignments, content area standards, and standardized tests. Just as specialized words are used in fields such as journalism, medicine, and law enforcement, academic vocabulary is the language of the classroom, school, and educational process. Recognizing these words and comprehending what they mean is, therefore, crucial to a student's academic success. The purpose of this book is to help students become familiar with the academic vocabulary most often used at their grade level. In this way, they will be better prepared to understand and complete classroom work, homework assignments, and tests.

Organized around curriculum areas and other common school topics, each four-page lesson introduces ten words and provides various ways for students to explore their meaning and usage. The lessons are intended as independent activities with some teacher support.

Materials

As you introduce the lessons, be sure to have the following items available:

Dictionaries
Thesauruses
Writing tools or computers
Student portfolios of written work

Tips for Using the Lessons

- Make a practice of using the lesson words often in classroom discussions and assignments. Call attention to these words as they come up.

- Consider having students make a set of word cards for each lesson. You might also make a class set and place it in your language arts center.

- Many words have more than one meaning, including some that are not given in the lesson. Point out additional meanings or invite students to discover and share them.

- Review parts of speech with students before each lesson. Many words can be used as more than one part of speech, including examples that are not given in this book. Encourage students to monitor their use of these words.

- Be sure to have students complete the Portfolio Page assignments on the second page of each lesson. Add your own writing assignments as well. Applying the lesson words in independent writing activities is essential in making the words part of students' vocabulary.

- Encourage students to consult more than one reference and to compare information.

 **TEXT** M E S S A G E You'll find a complete alphabetized list of all the lesson words in the Word List at the back of the book. Each page number listed identifies the first page of the lesson in which the word is found.

Lesson Organization

Each lesson is four pages long and introduces ten academic words.

The first lesson page includes:

lesson words

statement of lesson focus

simple sentences explaining meaning of words

cloze exercise

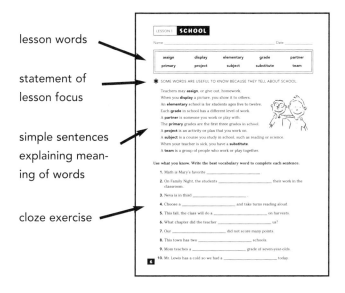

The second page includes:

lesson words

one or more exercises focusing on meaning

Portfolio Page writing assignment

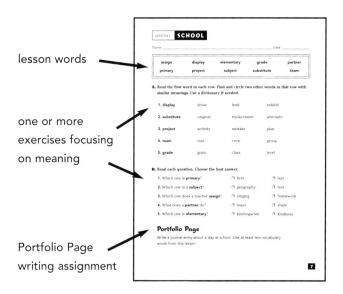

The third page includes:

lesson words

two or three exercises focusing on suffixes, prefixes, other meanings, parts of speech, word roots, or word structure

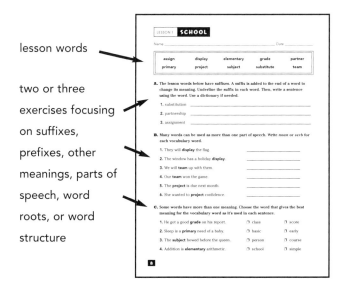

The fourth page includes:

a puzzle, game, maze, or other learning activity using the words

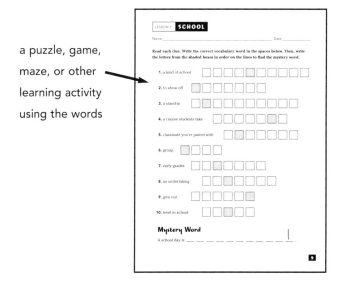

SCHOOL

Name _____ Date _____

---

assign	display	elementary	grade	partner
primary	project	subject	substitute	team

✱ SOME WORDS ARE USEFUL TO KNOW BECAUSE THEY TELL ABOUT SCHOOL.

Teachers may **assign**, or give out, homework.

When you **display** a picture, you show it to others.

An **elementary** school is for students ages five to twelve.

Each **grade** in school has a different level of work.

A **partner** is someone you work or play with.

The **primary** grades are the first three grades in school.

A **project** is an activity or plan that you work on.

A **subject** is a course you study in school, such as reading or science.

When your teacher is sick, you have a **substitute**.

A **team** is a group of people who work or play together.

Use what you know. Write the best vocabulary word to complete each sentence.

1. Math is Mary's favorite _____ .

2. On Family Night, the students _____ their work in the classroom.

3. Neva is in third _____ .

4. Choose a _____ and take turns reading aloud.

5. This fall, the class will do a _____ on harvests.

6. What chapter did the teacher _____ us?

7. Our _____ did not score many points.

8. This town has two _____ schools.

9. Mom teaches a _____ grade of seven-year-olds.

10. Mr. Lewis has a cold so we had a _____ today.

180 Essential Vocabulary Words for 3rd Grade © 2009 by Linda Ward Beech, Scholastic Teaching Resources

Name _____ Date _____

assign	display	elementary	grade	partner
primary	project	subject	substitute	team

A. Read the first word in each row. Find and circle two other words in that row with similar meanings. Use a dictionary if needed.

1. **display**   show   lend   exhibit

2. **substitute**   original   replacement   alternate

3. **project**   activity   mistake   plan

4. **team**   tear   crew   group

5. **grade**   grain   class   level

B. Read each question. Choose the best answer.

1. Which one is **primary**?   ❑ first   ❑ last

2. Which one is a **subject**?   ❑ geography   ❑ test

3. Which one does a teacher **assign**?   ❑ singing   ❑ homework

4. What does a **partner** do?   ❑ tease   ❑ share

5. Which one is **elementary**?   ❑ kindergarten   ❑ kindness

Portfolio Page

Write a journal entry about a day at school. Use at least two vocabulary words from this lesson.

180 Essential Vocabulary Words for 3rd Grade © 2009 by Linda Ward Beech, Scholastic Teaching Resources

Name _____ Date _____

assign	display	elementary	grade	partner
primary	project	subject	substitute	team

A. The lesson words below have suffixes. A suffix is added to the end of a word to change its meaning. Underline the suffix in each word. Then, write a sentence using the word. Use a dictionary if needed.

1. substitution _____

2. partnership _____

3. assignment _____

B. Many words can be used as more than one part of speech. Write *noun* or *verb* for each vocabulary word.

1. They will **display** the flag. _____

2. The window has a holiday **display**. _____

3. We will **team** up with them. _____

4. Our **team** won the game. _____

5. The **project** is due next month. _____

6. She wanted to **project** confidence. _____

C. Some words have more than one meaning. Choose the word that gives the best meaning for the vocabulary word as it's used in each sentence.

1. He got a good **grade** on his report. ❑ class ❑ score

2. Sleep is a **primary** need of a baby. ❑ basic ❑ early

3. The **subject** bowed before the queen. ❑ person ❑ course

4. Addition is **elementary** arithmetic. ❑ school ❑ simple

180 Essential Vocabulary Words for 3rd Grade © 2009 by Linda Ward Beech, Scholastic Teaching Resources

Name _____ Date _____

Read each clue. Write the correct vocabulary word in the spaces below. Then, write the letters from the shaded boxes in order on the lines to find the mystery word.

1. a kind of school

2. to show off

3. a stand-in

4. a course students take

5. classmate you're paired with

6. group

7. early grades

8. an undertaking

9. give out

10. level in school

Mystery Word

A school day is ___ ___ ___ ___ ___ ___ ___ ___ ___ ___ ___ .

180 Essential Vocabulary Words for 3rd Grade © 2009 by Linda Ward Beech, Scholastic Teaching Resources

Name _____ Date _____

author	character	detail	dialogue	fiction
paragraph	period	plot	series	setting

✳ YOU USE CERTAIN WORDS WHEN YOU TALK ABOUT READING.

An **author** is a person who writes a book.

A **character** is a person or animal in a story.

A **detail** tells you more about something.

When characters talk to each other, it is called **dialogue**.

A story about things that aren't real is **fiction**.

A **paragraph** is a group of sentences about the same idea.

A **period** is a punctuation mark at the end of a sentence.

The actions that unfold in a story make up the **plot**.

Books about the same characters are part of a **series**.

The **setting** is the place where a story happens.

Use what you know. Write the best vocabulary word to complete each sentence.

1. *Mrs. Piggle-Wiggle* is a book of _____ .

2. The _____ for *Sarah, Plain and Tall* is a farm on a prairie.

3. Jessie is one _____ in *The Boxcar Children*.

4. The _____ of *How to Eat Fried Worms* is Thomas Rockwell.

5. Nelson has read all the books in the _____ about
Encyclopedia Brown.

6. The _____ of the story was full of action.

7. Stop when you come to the _____ at the end of a sentence.

8. The first _____ on this page is very exciting.

9. Some of the _____ in this book is in Spanish.

10. Each _____ the author included about the funny car made us giggle.

180 Essential Vocabulary Words for 3rd Grade © 2009 by Linda Ward Beech, Scholastic Teaching Resources

Name _____ Date _____

author	character	detail	dialogue	fiction
paragraph	period	plot	series	setting

A. Read the riddle clues. Write a vocabulary word for each clue.

1. I am where a story takes place. What am I? _____

2. I am someone in a story. What am I? _____

3. I am what someone says in a book. What am I? _____

4. I am what happens in a story. What am I? _____

5. I am a group of several related books. What am I? _____

6. I write stories. What am I? _____

B. Read each question. Choose the best answer.

1. Which one is **fiction**? ❏ nonfiction ❏ make-believe

2. Where is a **period**? ❏ end ❏ middle

3. What does a **detail** add? ❏ information ❏ addition

4. Which one is in a **paragraph**? ❏ parachute ❏ sentence

Portfolio Page

Write a response to a book you have read. Tell what your favorite part is and why. Use at least two vocabulary words from this lesson.

180 Essential Vocabulary Words for 3rd Grade © 2009 by Linda Ward Beech, Scholastic Teaching Resources

Name _____ Date _____

author	character	detail	dialogue	fiction
paragraph	period	plot	series	setting

A. The lesson words below have suffixes. A suffix is added to the end of a word to change its meaning. Underline the suffix in each word. Then, write a sentence using the word. Use a dictionary if needed.

1. authority _____

2. fictional _____

3. serial _____

4. characteristic _____

B. Some words have more than one meaning. Choose the word or phrase that gives the best meaning for the vocabulary word as it's used in each sentence.

1. They grew flowers on the small **plot**. ❒ lot ❒ story events

2. It was a happy **period** in her life. ❒ time ❒ punctuation mark

3. He put a fork at each **setting**. ❒ place at a table ❒ place of a story

4. Sam worked on guard **detail**. ❒ another fact ❒ duty

C. For each vocabulary word below, read the Greek and Latin word root and its meanings. Then, write another word with the same root.

1. The Greek root *graph*, as in **paragraph**, means "to write." _____

2. The Latin root *dia*, as in **dialogue**, means "over or across." _____

Name _____ Date _____

Read the clues. Then, complete the puzzle using vocabulary words from this lesson.

Across

2. a book about make-believe things

6. words that book characters say

7. a group of sentences about the same idea

8. the place where a story happens

9. a punctuation mark

Down

1. the main events of a story

3. a person in a story

4. a small piece of information about something

5. a person who writes a book

8. several books about the same characters

180 Essential Vocabulary Words for 3rd Grade © 2009 by Linda Ward Beech, Scholastic Teaching Resources

Name _____ Date _____

audience	**brainstorm**	**draft**	**edit**	**journal**
outline	**proofread**	**publish**	**report**	**revise**

✳ YOU USE CERTAIN WORDS WHEN YOU TALK ABOUT WRITING.

People who read what you write are your **audience**.

When you **brainstorm**, you think of things to write about.

A **draft** is a first try at writing something.

You **edit** your work to make sure it is just right.

A **journal** is a notebook for writing ideas.

An **outline** helps you organize what you are writing.

To be sure there are no spelling mistakes, **proofread** your work.

You present or **publish** your writing to share it with others.

A **report** gives information about a topic.

A partner can help you **revise** or change your work to improve it.

features   habitat

PANDA

enemies   food

Use what you know. Write the best vocabulary word to complete each sentence.

1. Gail has to write a _____ for science.

2. She will _____ topics to write about.

3. Her _____ is a good place to jot down ideas.

4. Gail makes an _____ to help her plan each paragraph.

5. Then she writes a first _____ .

6. Her teacher and classmates will be Gail's _____ .

7. First, Raul helps Gail to _____ her work.

8. Next, she will _____ her final piece so it is the way she wants it.

9. Are there spelling errors? If so, Gail will _____ to correct them.

14 **10.** Finally, it is time to _____ her report.

Name _____ Date _____

audience	brainstorm	draft	edit	journal
outline	proofread	publish	report	revise

A. Read the words at the base of each arc. Then write the best vocabulary word along the arc.

1.

    plan   framework

2.

    readers   listeners

3.

    account   information

4.

    diary   notebook

B. Read each question about writing. Choose the best answer.

1. What is a **draft**?   ❏ best effort   ❏ first try

2. Why do you **revise**?   ❏ ruin   ❏ improve

3. When do you **proofread**?   ❏ end   ❏ beginning

4. Why do you **publish**?   ❏ punish   ❏ share

C. Underline the best ending for each sentence.

1. He needs to **edit** his paper so it will be _____ .

    a. messy   **b.** perfect   **c.** long

2. They wanted to **brainstorm** to _____ .

    a. explore ideas   **b.** amuse themselves   **c.** check their work

Portfolio Page

Write an e-mail that a peer editor might send to a classmate about his or her story. Use at least two vocabulary words from this lesson.

Name _____ Date _____

audience	brainstorm	draft	edit	journal
outline	proofread	publish	report	revise

A. When two small words are put together into one word, it is called a compound word. Use these words to make three compound lesson words.

storm   line   proof   brain   read   out

1. _____

2. _____

3. _____

B. Some words have more than one meaning. Choose the word or phrase that gives the best meaning for the vocabulary word as it's used in each sentence.

1. Put on a sweater if you feel a **draft**.   ❏ slight breeze   ❏ early version

2. They had an **audience** with the king.   ❏ reader   ❏ meeting

C. The lesson words below have suffixes. A suffix is added to the end of a word to change its meaning. Underline the suffix in each word. Then, write a sentence using the word. Use a dictionary if needed.

1. journalist   _____

2. revision   _____

3. editor   _____

4. reporter   _____

5. publisher   _____

180 Essential Vocabulary Words for 3rd Grade © 2009 by Linda Ward Beech, Scholastic Teaching Resources

Name _____ Date _____

Read the clues. Identify the correct vocabulary word and write it next to its clue. Then find and circle each word in the puzzle.

C	T	P	R	O	O	F	R	E	A	D	D	F	B
W	B	U	J	O	U	R	N	A	L	G	I	K	R
H	M	B	Q	V	T	L	S	C	X	R	N	P	A
A	F	L	X	R	L	U	E	H	S	E	C	W	I
E	D	I	T	Z	I	C	R	K	M	P	D	V	N
T	G	S	N	R	N	K	E	Q	E	O	J	O	S
I	S	H	F	J	E	I	V	U	D	R	A	F	T
K	P	C	N	T	Z	G	I	R	Q	T	A	T	O
Y	L	A	E	M	Y	I	S	L	R	U	J	Z	R
D	S	M	A	U	D	I	E	N	C	E	O	H	M

Hint:
The words
can run
ACROSS
or
DOWN.

Clues

1. to read carefully for mistakes in spelling _____

2. a place in which you write responses to things _____

3. what editors do _____

4. one version of your writing _____

5. people who will read your writing _____

6. to present your work _____

7. a way to organize information _____

8. a way to find a topic for writing _____

9. a research paper about a topic _____

10. to reread and make changes if needed _____

180 Essential Vocabulary Words for 3rd Grade © 2009 by Linda Ward Beech, Scholastic Teaching Resources

TEXTBOOKS

Name _____ Date _____

caption	chapter	feature	heading	index
inform	main	quote	text	topic

✳ YOU USE CERTAIN WORDS WHEN YOU TALK ABOUT A TEXTBOOK.

A **caption** tells what a picture is about.

A **chapter** is a division, or part, of a textbook.

A **feature** is a special or extra article in a textbook.

A **heading** is a kind of title.

An **index** is at the back of the book and lists what is in the book.

Our textbooks **inform** or tell us about different subjects.

The most important idea in a paragraph is the **main** idea.

A **quote** contains someone's exact words.

The reading matter in a book is called the **text**.

A **topic** is a subject.

> "We're lost!" cried Kirk.

*A **quote** has quotation marks around it.*

Use what you know. Write the best vocabulary word to complete each sentence.

1. Today, the class will read the first _____ in the textbook.

2. The _____ in large type tells what this section is about.

3. The _____ of today's assignment is animals.

4. Does the book _____ readers about insects, too?

5. Can you find the _____ idea in this paragraph?

6. This book has both _____ and pictures.

7. To learn about this photo, read the _____ .

8. Use the _____ to find the page where it tells about tigers.

9. Then read the special _____ on tiger cubs.

10. This _____ tells what the zookeeper said.

180 Essential Vocabulary Words for 3rd Grade © 2009 by Linda Ward Beech, Scholastic Teaching Resources

TEXTBOOKS

Name _____ Date _____

caption	chapter	feature	heading	index
inform	main	quote	text	topic

A. Underline the best ending for each sentence.

1. The **index** helps you find information _____ .

    a. slowly   **b.** neatly   **c.** easily

2. The **heading** for each section is a kind of _____ .

    a. quiz   **b.** summary   **c.** paragraph

3. Each **chapter** makes a textbook easier to use by _____ .

    a. organizing information   **b.** asking questions   **c.** giving opinions

4. She read the **caption** under the picture so she could _____ .

    a. write a story   **b.** learn more   **c.** turn the page

5. Adding the **quote** given by the senator made the text more _____ .

    a. unreal   **b.** fictional   **c.** believable

B. Read each question. Choose the best answer.

1. Which one is **main**?   ❐ common   ❐ important

2. What do you do with **text**?   ❐ read it   ❐ solve it

3. Which one is a **feature**?   ❐ chapter   ❐ column

4. Which one is a **topic**?   ❐ index   ❐ insects

Portfolio Page

Write about a fact or idea you have learned from a textbook. Use at least two vocabulary words from this lesson.

TEXTBOOKS

Name _____ Date _____

caption	chapter	feature	heading	index
inform	main	quote	text	topic

A. Some words have more than one meaning. Choose the word that gives the best meaning for the vocabulary word as it's used in each sentence.

1. The workers are repairing the water **main**.   ❐ pipe   ❐ major

2. He belongs to the local **chapter** of that club.   ❐ pages   ❐ branch

3. This TV show has **captions**.   ❐ subtitles   ❐ details

4. She pointed her **index** finger at us.   ❐ list   ❐ forefinger

B. Many words can be used as more than one part of speech. Write *noun* or *verb* for each underlined word.

1. The cows are **heading** this way.   _____

2. Read the **heading** of each section.   _____

3. The seller will **quote** you a price.   _____

4. That is a **quote** from Harry Potter.   _____

5. What **feature** do you like best?   _____

6. The show will **feature** singers.   _____

C. The lesson words below have suffixes. A suffix is added to the end of each word to change its meaning. Underline the suffix in each word. Then, write a sentence using the word. Use a dictionary if needed.

1. information   _____

2. texture   _____

3. topical   _____

TEXTBOOKS

Name _____ Date _____

Write a vocabulary word that belongs with each group of words.

1. _____

photo

picture

map

2. _____

thought

idea

paragraph

3. _____

pages

list

alphabetical

4. _____

information

content

subject

5. _____

tell

explain

disclose

6. _____

part

section

portion

7. _____

words

read

book

8. _____

speaker

said

passage

9. _____

name

title

headline

10. _____

article

extra

special

Name _____ Date _____

| area | chart | estimate | graph | measure |
| order | pattern | plus | solve | sum |

✱ YOU USE CERTAIN WORDS WHEN YOU TALK ABOUT MATH.

You find the **area** of a space by multiplying its length and width.

A **chart** organizes information to present it in a clear way.

An **estimate** is an opinion or judgment about amount or size.

A **graph** is a kind of chart that shows facts over time.

When you **measure** something, you find its size or weight.

Order is the way things are arranged.

A **pattern** is a design that is repeated many times.

Plus means "added to."

If you **solve** a problem, you figure out the answer.

When you add numbers, you get a **sum**.

Use what you know. Write the best vocabulary word to complete each sentence.

1. The _____ shows that there are more people now than last year.

2. Luke put the boxes in _____ by size.

3. Judy's parents _____ her height every year on her birthday.

4. Shelly keeps a _____ showing which chores she has done.

5. The _____ of 3 and 6 is 9.

6. There are 25 students on the bus _____ the teacher.

7. The boys gave us an _____ of how much paper we need.

8. Sid looked for a _____ in the design.

9. How would you find the _____ of the room?

10. We have five problems to _____ for homework.

180 Essential Vocabulary Words for 3rd Grade © 2009 by Linda Ward Beech, Scholastic Teaching Resources

MATH

Name _____ Date _____

area	chart	estimate	graph	measure
order	pattern	plus	solve	sum

A. **Read each question. Choose the best answer.**

1. What do you **solve**?   ❑ program   ❑ problem

2. What is a **plus** sign for?   ❑ subtraction ❑ addition

3. What is an **estimate**?   ❑ plan   ❑ guess

4. What is a **chart** for?   ❑ organize   ❑ chat

5. What does a **graph** show?   ❑ display   ❑ change

B. **Write a sentence to answer each question. Use a vocabulary word in your sentence.**

1. How can you find the length of a box? _____

_____

2. How can you find how much land a football field covers? _____

_____

3. What do you call a repeating design? _____

_____

4. What is the total of an addition problem? _____

_____

5. What does it mean when you arrange something? _____

_____

Portfolio Page

Write a math word problem for a classmate to solve. Use at least two
vocabulary words from this lesson.

Name _____ Date _____

area	chart	estimate	graph	measure
order	pattern	plus	solve	sum

A. Some words have more than one meaning. Choose the word that gives the best meaning for the vocabulary word as it's used in each sentence.

1. The teacher will **sum** up the lesson. ❒ add ❒ summarize

2. Her **area** of interest was art. ❒ field ❒ space

3. They took several **measures** to make the school safe. ❒ sizes ❒ steps

4. He will **order** pizza from the shop. ❒ request ❒ arrange

5. The children traced bears from a **pattern**. ❒ description ❒ model

B. A prefix is added to the beginning of a word to change its meaning. The underlined words in the sentences below begin with the prefix *un-*. Read each sentence, then write what the word means. Use a dictionary if needed.

1. That problem is <u>unsolved</u>.

_____

2. The ship sailed into <u>uncharted</u> waters.

_____

C. Each of these words is found in one of the vocabulary words. Write the vocabulary word on the line.

1. mate _____

2. rap _____

3. us _____

180 Essential Vocabulary Words for 3rd Grade © 2009 by Linda Ward Beech, Scholastic Teaching Resources

Name _____ Date _____

Read the first word in each row. Find and circle the word in each group that doesn't belong. Then, in order, write the words you circled to make a silly sentence.

1. sum	total	amount	some
2. measure	markets	inch	weigh
3. chart	carry	table	list
4. order	organize	arrange	orange
5. area	place	space	lace
6. pattern	repeat	plain	design
7. solve	socks	answer	explain
8. estimate	judgment	enormous	guess
9. plus	add	more	plums
10. graph	chart	trend	grapes

Silly Sentence

_____ _____ _____

_____ _____ , _____

_____ , _____ _____ ,

and _____ .

180 Essential Vocabulary Words for 3rd Grade © 2009 by Linda Ward Beech, Scholastic Teaching Resources

Name _____ Date _____

| culture | disaster | event | export | job |
| leisure | population | tradition | transport | trend |

✱ SOME WORDS ARE USED OFTEN IN SOCIAL STUDIES.

Culture is the way of life of a group of people.

A **disaster** is something that causes suffering and pain.

An **event** is something that happens.

When you **export** things, you sell them to other countries.

People work at a **job**.

Your spare time is your **leisure** time.

The number of people living in a place is its **population**.

A **tradition** is a custom that people pass down.

When you carry something from one place to another, you **transport** it.

People often follow a **trend**, or way of thinking or acting.

Use what you know. Write the best vocabulary word to complete each sentence.

1. The _____ of that town grows each year.

2. The train wreck was a terrible _____ .

3. In his _____ time, Terry likes to read mysteries.

4. We studied the _____ of some Native American groups.

5. Dina has a _____ working at the store.

6. It is a _____ in our family to make holiday cookies.

7. One new _____ is to buy prepared food.

8. The boys had to _____ their bikes over the stream.

9. A reporter attended the play and wrote about the _____ .

10. This company will _____ the shoes it makes to Spain.

180 Essential Vocabulary Words for 3rd Grade © 2009 by Linda Ward Beech, Scholastic Teaching Resources

SOCIAL STUDIES

Name _____ Date _____

culture	disaster	event	export	job
leisure	population	tradition	transport	trend

A. Read the first word in each row. Find and circle two other words in that row with similar meanings. Use a dictionary if needed.

1. event	promise	happening	occasion
2. job	work	task	joke
3. transport	carry	celebrate	move
4. leisure	leftover	spare	free
5. disaster	accident	distance	wreck
6. trend	fad	direction	terrific

B. Read each question. Choose the best answer.

1. What does an **export** do? ❐ enter ❐ exit
2. Which one describes a **tradition**? ❐ repeated ❐ once
3. Which one is **population**? ❐ popular ❐ people
4. What is part of **culture**? ❐ weather ❐ beliefs

Portfolio Page

Write a story for a newspaper telling about a school event. Use at least two vocabulary words from this lesson.

180 Essential Vocabulary Words for 3rd Grade © 2009 by Linda Ward Beech, Scholastic Teaching Resources

SOCIAL STUDIES

Name _____ Date _____

culture	disaster	event	export	job
leisure	population	tradition	transport	trend

A. Complete each sentence using two vocabulary words.

1. Her _____ took so many hours each day that she didn't

have much _____ time.

2. An _____ takes place at one certain time, but a

_____ develops over a period of time.

3. A flood or other _____ can affect the

_____ of a community.

4. A _____ of holding a special feast each year might be part

of a group's _____ .

5. When you _____ goods to another country, you must find

a way to _____ them to that place.

B. Follow the directions to write the words.

1. Write the lesson words that end in -*port*.

_____   _____

2. Write the lesson words that end in -*tion*.

_____   _____

3. Write one of these suffixes on the words below to change their meaning:

-*ous*, -*y*, -*ful*, -*ly*.

trend_____   event_____   leisure_____

180 Essential Vocabulary Words for 3rd Grade © 2009 by Linda Ward Beech, Scholastic Teaching Resources

SOCIAL STUDIES

Name _____ Date _____

Read the clues. Then, complete the puzzle using vocabulary words from this lesson.

Across

1. something that takes place or occurs

3. rhymes with *friend*

5. free time

7. shared way of life

9. a car, boat, or airplane can do this

10. a group of people that make up a community

Down

2. the opposite of *import*

4. a flood is an example

6. something families often have

8. a way to earn money

Name _____ Date _____

address	**globe**	**key**	**label**	**locate**
overseas	**region**	**resource**	**route**	**symbol**

✱ SOME WORDS ARE USEFUL TO KNOW BECAUSE THEY ARE USED WITH MAPS.

An **address** tells where you live.

A small model of Earth is a **globe**.

Use the **key** to find out what things on a map mean.

A **label** on a map identifies a place.

A map helps you **locate** or find a place.

Overseas means "in another country or continent."

A large area is called a **region**.

A map can show where a **resource**, such as coal, is found.

Drivers use maps to find a **route** from one place to another.

A **symbol** is a picture that stands for something else.

Use what you know. Write the best vocabulary word to complete each sentence.

1. Mr. Stone keeps a _____ of the world near his desk.

2. When he has a vacation, he hopes to travel _____ .

3. He'd like to visit a certain _____ in Italy.

4. He has the _____ of a hotel there.

5. The _____ helps Mr. Stone understand the map he bought.

6. One _____ stands for interesting places to see.

7. Another stands for an important natural _____ .

8. Each _____ is in English so Mr. Stone can use the map easily.

9. This weekend, Mr. Stone will _____ all the places on the map he wants to see.

10. Then, he can carefully plan the _____ he will take.

180 Essential Vocabulary Words for 3rd Grade © 2009 by Linda Ward Beech, Scholastic Teaching Resources

Name _____ Date _____

address	globe	key	label	locate
overseas	region	resource	route	symbol

A. Read each pair of words. Write the related vocabulary word on the line.

1. symbolize   symbolic   _____

2. location   relocate   _____

3. global   globetrot   _____

4. keyhole   keynote   _____

5. regional   regionally   _____

B. Read each question. Choose the best answer.

1. Which one is **overseas**?   ❏ water   ❏ country

2. What is an **address**?   ❏ person   ❏ place

3. What is a **label** for?   ❏ information   ❏ confusion

4. Which one is a **route**?   ❏ road   ❏ routine

5. What is a **resource**?   ❏ useful   ❏ useless

Portfolio Page

Write about a way you can use a map. Use at least two vocabulary words from this lesson.

180 Essential Vocabulary Words for 3rd Grade © 2009 by Linda Ward Beech, Scholastic Teaching Resources

Name _____ Date _____

| address | globe | key | label | locate |
| overseas | region | resource | route | symbol |

A. Some words have more than one meaning. Choose the word or phrase that gives the best meaning for the vocabulary word as it's used in each sentence.

1. He will **address** the audience. ❐ write to ❐ speak to

2. The **key** will open the door. ❐ turn lock ❐ explain symbols

3. She used her **resources**
to get out of a jam. ❐ minerals ❐ skills

4. A lightbulb is a **globe**. ❐ model of Earth ❐ sphere or ball

5. Those are **overseas** packages. ❐ foreign ❐ place

B. Many words can be used as more than one part of speech. Write *noun* or *verb* for each vocabulary word.

1. Please **label** your drawing. _____

2. Add a **label** to show the capital city. _____

3. We need to read the signs that
will **route** us to a detour. _____

4. The bus took the same **route** every day. _____

C. Read the word meaning in each sentence. Then, write the vocabulary word that comes from the Greek or Latin word.

1. The Latin word *regio* means "direction." _____

2. The Greek word *symbolon* means "sign." _____

3. The Latin word *locus* means "place." _____

180 Essential Vocabulary Words for 3rd Grade © 2009 by Linda Ward Beech, Scholastic Teaching Resources

SOCIAL STUDIES/MAP SKILLS

Name _____ Date _____

Play the Word Clue Game.

Read the clues. Write the best vocabulary word for each clue. Use each word only once.

Clues	Vocabulary Words
1. the opposite of *lose*	
2. sounds like *cymbal*	
3. means the same as *path*	
4. has the same letters as the name Bella	
5. contains the word *sour*	
6. rhymes with *robe*	
7. opposite of *underseas*	
8. means the same as *area*	
9. rhymes with *tea*	
10. contains the word *dress*	

Name _____ Date _____

absorb	**adapt**	**conservation**	**energy**	**environment**
habitat	**launch**	**migrate**	**survive**	**technology**

✳ SOME WORDS ARE USED OFTEN IN SCIENCE.

Absorb means to soak up.

If you **adapt** something, you change it.

Saving trees is a form of **conservation**.

You need a lot of **energy** to run a race.

Your surroundings are your **environment**.

A **habitat** is a place where a plant or animal lives.

When you **launch** something, you put it in motion.

Animals that **migrate** move from place to place.

A plant needs water to **survive**.

The use of scientific knowledge is **technology**.

Use what you know. Write the best vocabulary word to complete each sentence.

1. Fuels provide _____ to heat buildings.

2. Clean air is important for our _____ .

3. When their _____ is destroyed, animals lose their homes.

4. People cannot _____ without food.

5. Many birds _____ to warmer places in winter.

6. A sponge will _____ water.

7. The scientists are ready to _____ the rocket.

8. People who care about _____ try not to waste resources.

9. Sometimes a plant has to _____ to new conditions.

10. The use of _____ has improved transportation.

180 Essential Vocabulary Words for 3rd Grade © 2009 by Linda Ward Beech, Scholastic Teaching Resources

Name _____ Date _____

absorb	adapt	conservation	energy	environment
habitat	launch	migrate	survive	technology

A. Read the word in the first column. Draw a line to match it with a word or phrase in the second column that has a similar meaning.

1. habitat   a. start

2. migrate   b. soak up

3. environment   c. move

4. launch   d. adjust

5. absorb   e. home

6. energy   f. surroundings

7. survive   g. power

8. adapt   h. live

B. Read each pair of words. Write the related vocabulary word on the line.

1.   technical   technological   _____

2.   conserve   conservancy   _____

Portfolio Page

Write a report about a plant or animal. Use at least two vocabulary words from this lesson.

Name _____ Date _____

absorb	adapt	conservation	energy	environment
habitat	launch	migrate	survive	technology

A. The lesson words below have suffixes. A suffix is added to the end of a word to change its meaning. Underline the suffix in each word below. Then, write a sentence using the word. Use a dictionary if needed.

1. survival _____

2. migration _____

3. energize _____

4. habitation _____

5. adaptation _____

B. Underline the best ending for each sentence.

1. To practice **conservation**, you might _____ .

    a. waste paper   **b.** lose paper   **c.** reuse paper

2. You **launch** a project by _____ .

    a. ending it   **b.** starting it   **c.** erasing it

3. When you **absorb** information, you _____ .

    a. help it   **b.** forget it   **c.** learn it

4. A healthy **environment** must have clean _____ .

    a. smoke   **b.** water   **c.** clothes

5. The purpose of **technology** is to _____ .

    a. improve things   **b.** harm things   **c.** ignore things

Name _____ Date _____

Read the clues. Then, complete the puzzle using vocabulary words from this lesson.

Across

4. preserving things

5. to take things in

6. set something in motion

8. power or strength

9. moving at a regular time

10. change to fit new conditions

Down

1. to stay alive

2. when science is put to practical use

3. the air, water, and other surroundings of living things

7. the area in which an animal lives

SCIENCE INQUIRY

Name _____ Date _____

affect	category	conclusion	demonstrate	discover
forecast	identify	inquire	preserve	review

✱ SOME WORDS ARE USED OFTEN IN SCIENCE.

If things **affect** you, they have an influence on you.

A **category** is a group.

A **conclusion** is a decision you make after thinking.

When you **demonstrate** something, you show how to do it.

If you find something for the first time, you **discover** it.

If you tell what may happen, you **forecast** it.

You **identify** something when you learn exactly what it is.

To **inquire** is to ask for information.

To **preserve** something is to keep it safe.

When you **review** something, you look at it again.

Use what you know. Write the best vocabulary word to complete each sentence.

1. We will _____ about our science project to find out what it will be.

2. Mr. Wiley will _____ how to do the experiment.

3. First we will _____ the problem.

4. How does heat _____ certain things?

5. That is what we want to _____ .

6. First we make a _____ for things that will melt. Then we make one for things that won't.

7. We _____ that heat will melt ice cream.

8. "When ice cream gets warm, you cannot _____ it," Sumi says.

9. We carefully _____ each step in our experiment.

10. Then we draw a _____ .

180 Essential Vocabulary Words for 3rd Grade © 2009 by Linda Ward Beech, Scholastic Teaching Resources

SCIENCE INQUIRY

Name _____ Date _____

affect	category	conclusion	demonstrate	discover
forecast	identify	inquire	preserve	review

A. For each number, read the three words. Use a colored pencil to shade the word in one of the bottom boxes that means the opposite of the word in top box.

1.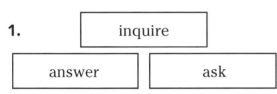

2.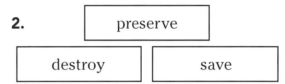

3.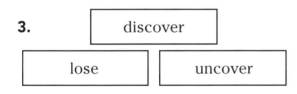

4.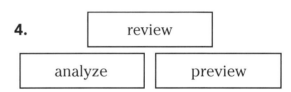

B. Read the words at the base of each arc. Then write the best vocabulary word along that arc.

1.
touch   impress

2.
class   group

3.
agreement   decision

4.
foretell   predict

5.
recognize   know

6.
prove   show

Portfolio Page

Write about a science experiment you have done. Use at least two vocabulary words from this lesson.

SCIENCE INQUIRY

Name _____ Date _____

affect	category	conclusion	demonstrate	discover
forecast	identify	inquire	preserve	review

A. The lesson words below have suffixes. A suffix is added to the end of a word to change its meaning. Underline the suffix in each word. Then, write a sentence using the word. Use a dictionary if needed.

1. affection _____

2. discovery _____

3. forecaster _____

B. Some words have more than one meaning. Choose the word that gives the best meaning for the vocabulary word as it's used in each sentence.

1. We clapped at the **conclusion** of the show.

     ❏ decision   ❏ ending

2. Toby wrote a book **review**.

     ❏ report   ❏ study

3. Many people plan to **demonstrate** against the price increase.

     ❏ explain something   ❏ show opinion

C. Each of these words is found in a vocabulary word. Write the vocabulary word on the line.

1. dent _____

2. serve _____

3. gory _____

4. ire _____

180 Essential Vocabulary Words for 3rd Grade © 2009 by Linda Ward Beech, Scholastic Teaching Resources

SCIENCE INQUIRY

Name _____ Date _____

Read each clue. Write the correct vocabulary word in the spaces below. Then, write the letters from the shaded boxes in order on the lines to find the mystery word.

1. to find out

2. to name someone

3. to look again

4. to protect

5. a decision

6. show how to
do something

7. to try to find out

8. a group

9. influence in some way

10. to predict

Mystery Word

Scientists ___ ___ ___ ___ ___ ___ ___ ___ ___ ___ _e__ to learn about
new things.

Name _____ Date _____

file	link	list	notes	plan
predict	recall	research	study	test

✳ SOME WORDS ARE USEFUL TO KNOW WHEN YOU ARE STUDYING.

A **file** is a place to store paper.

A **link** joins or connects things.

A series of items is a **list**.

Notes are short written records.

A **plan** is an idea about what to do that is thought out ahead of time.

If you **predict** something, you tell about it in advance.

When you **recall** information, you remember it.

You do **research** to learn about a topic.

You **study** a subject to gain information.

A **test** is an exam.

Use what you know. Write the best vocabulary word to complete each sentence.

1. Our teacher gave the class tips on how to _____ for a quiz.

2. Ron made a numbered _____ of the tips.

3. One tip was to make a _____ .

4. Another was to take _____ in class.

5. Nicki tries to _____ what questions will be asked.

6. Bart tries to _____ what he reads to what he already knows.

7. After she reads a paragraph, Cindy stops to _____ the main points.

8. Ling keeps his papers in a _____ .

9. These tips are helpful when students have a _____ , too.

10. Next week, we will get tips on how to do _____ for a report.

180 Essential Vocabulary Words for 3rd Grade © 2009 by Linda Ward Beech, Scholastic Teaching Resources

STUDY SKILLS

Name _____ Date _____

file	**link**	**list**	**notes**	**plan**
predict	**recall**	**research**	**study**	**test**

A. Read each question. Choose the best answer.

1. What does a **link** do? ❐ correct ❐ connect

2. What is a **file** for? ❐ organize ❐ organic

3. What can you **recall**? ❐ past ❐ future

4. What do you **study**? ❐ lessen ❐ lesson

5. What are in **notes**? ❐ words ❐ worms

6. What is a **list** for? ❐ forgetting ❐ remembering

7. What does a **test** do? ❐ check ❐ cheer

B. Write a sentence to answer each question.

1. Why would you make a **plan**? _____
   _____

2. Why would you do **research**? _____
   _____

3. When might you **predict** something? _____
   _____

Portfolio Page

Write some tips about good study habits. Use at least two vocabulary words from this lesson.

Name _____ Date _____

file	link	list	notes	plan
predict	recall	research	study	test

A. Some words have more than one meaning. Choose the word or phrase that gives the best meaning for the vocabulary word in each sentence.

1. We walked in single **file**.   ❐ folder   ❐ line

2. The ship began to **list**.   ❐ lean   ❐ items in order

3. She sang all of the high **notes**.   ❐ records   ❐ sounds

4. The company had to **recall** some cars.   ❐ remember   ❐ take back

5. They sat in the **study** to talk.   ❐ room   ❐ learn

B. Many words can be used as more than one part of speech. Circle *noun* or *verb* for each vocabulary word.

1. Jess wanted to **link** the two ideas.   noun   verb

2. The chain had a weak **link**.   noun   verb

3. Here is a **plan** of the building.   noun   verb

4. Mary will **plan** the party.   noun   verb

5. This exercise will **test** your strength.   noun   verb

6. The students had a spelling **test**.   noun   verb

C. The lesson words below have suffixes. A suffix is added to the end of a word to change its meaning. Underline the suffix in each word. Then, write a sentence using the word. Use a dictionary if needed.

1. researcher _____

2. prediction _____

180 Essential Vocabulary Words for 3rd Grade © 2009 by Linda Ward Beech, Scholastic Teaching Resources

STUDY SKILLS

Name _____ Date _____

Read the first word in each row. Find and circle the word that means almost the same thing. Use the answers to help you find your way through the maze.

1. file	mess	storage	fail
2. link	jolt	line	join
3. list	inventory	last	lost
4. note	record	song	not
5. plan	plane	program	share
6. predict	review	present	forecast
7. recall	remind	forget	remember
8. research	search	resource	reward
9. study	student	learn	class
10. test	tell	exam	grade

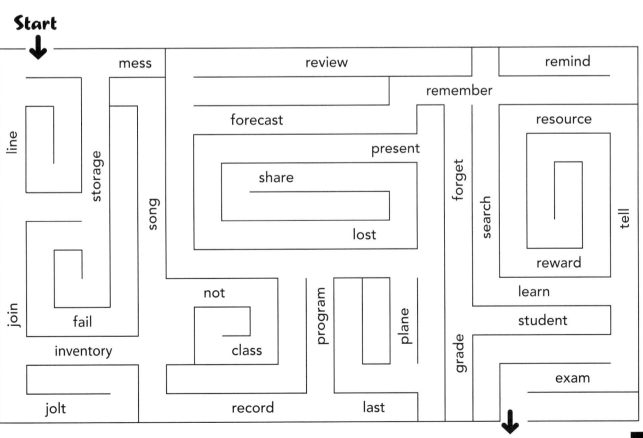

Name _____ Date _____

create	design	draw	exhibit	form
illustrate	pose	style	trace	visual

✳ SOME WORDS ARE USED OFTEN IN ART.

When you **create** something, you make it.

A **design** is a pattern or plan.

You **draw** a picture with a pencil.

If you **exhibit** something, you display it.

The **form** of something is its shape.

When you **illustrate** something, you make it clearer with a picture.

If you **pose** for a picture, you model for it.

Style is a certain way of doing something.

When you **trace** a line, you copy it.

Visual means having to do with seeing.

Use what you know. Write the best vocabulary word to complete each sentence.

1. Mandy tried to _____ her dog with a pencil.

2. She planned to use the picture to _____ a story about him.

3. She studied the _____ of Buddy's head.

4. But Buddy moved around and would not _____ for her.

5. Mandy had to _____ her picture another way.

6. She decided to _____ Buddy's head from a photo.

7. She used a blue and white _____ for a border.

8. It had a good _____ effect.

9. Mandy wanted to _____ her picture and story in a show.

10. She was proud to display the realistic _____ of her work.

180 Essential Vocabulary Words for 3rd Grade © 2009 by Linda Ward Beech, Scholastic Teaching Resources

Name _____ Date _____

create	**design**	**draw**	**exhibit**	**form**
illustrate	**pose**	**style**	**trace**	**visual**

A. For each number, read the three words. Use a colored pencil to shade the word in one of the bottom boxes that means the opposite of the word in top box.

1.

form

shape	formless

2.

create

destroy	make

3.

exhibit

show	hide

4.

trace

copy	erase

B. Read each question. Choose the best answer.

1. Which one is like **draw**?   ❐ sketch   ❐ scratch

2. Which one is **visual**?   ❐ song   ❐ sign

3. Which one can **pose**?   ❐ medal   ❐ model

4. Which one has got **style**?   ❐ fashion   ❐ fasten

5. Which one is a **design**?   ❐ competition   ❐ composition

6. Which one can **illustrate** a picture?   ❐ artist   ❐ author

Portfolio Page

Describe a painting or other work of art that you like. Use at least two vocabulary words from this lesson.

180 Essential Vocabulary Words for 3rd Grade © 2009 by Linda Ward Beech, Scholastic Teaching Resources

Name _____ Date _____

create	design	draw	exhibit	form
illustrate	pose	style	trace	visual

A. These words have suffixes. A suffix is added to the end of a word to change its meaning. Underline the suffix in each word below. Then, write a sentence using the word. Use a dictionary if needed.

1. creation _____

2. designer _____

3. illustration _____

3. exhibition _____

4. stylist _____

5. visually _____

B. A prefix is added to the beginning of a word to change its meaning. These words have the prefix *re-*. It means "again." Write a sentence using each word.

1. redraw _____

2. retrace _____

3. reform _____

C. Complete the poem with a vocabulary word that rhymes.

Could you stand on your toes

To _____ with a rose?

Who knows?

180 Essential Vocabulary Words for 3rd Grade © 2009 by Linda Ward Beech, Scholastic Teaching Resources

Name _____ Date _____

Play the Word Clue Game.

Read the clues. Write the best vocabulary word for each clue. Use each word only once.

Clues	Vocabulary Words
1. has the same letters as *crate*	
2. rhymes with *warm*	
3. means the same as *invent*	
4. has the word *sign* in it	
5. is related to the word *visualize*	
6. is *ward* spelled backward	
7. can also mean "give an example"	
8. means "get in position"	
9. has the word *bit* in it	
10. rhymes with *while*	

TESTS

Name _____ Date _____

compare	complete	define	describe	discuss
example	instructions	passage	respond	score

✱ SOME WORDS APPEAR OFTEN ON TESTS.

When you **compare** things, you show how they are alike and different.

If you **complete** something, you finish it.

Define means "make something clear."

By telling what something is like, you **describe** it.

If you talk something over with others, you **discuss** it.

One thing that shows what others are like is an **example**.

Instructions tell how to do something.

A **passage** is a short piece from a written work.

When you **respond**, you answer.

A **score** is the grade you get on a test.

Use what you know. Write the best vocabulary word to complete each sentence.

1. Before a test, our teacher will _____ the material with us.

2. He reminds us to read the _____ carefully.

3. We may have to _____ to different types of questions.

4. Sometimes an _____ is given to help us.

5. Some tests ask us to _____ a sentence.

6. Often we have to read a short _____ first.

7. Sometimes we are asked to _____ two things.

8. For vocabulary tests, we have to _____ words.

9. For a reading test, we might _____ a character.

10. We try to improve our _____ on each test.

180 Essential Vocabulary Words for 3rd Grade © 2009 by Linda Ward Beech, Scholastic Teaching Resources

Name _____ Date _____

compare	complete	define	describe	discuss
example	instructions	passage	respond	score

A. Read the first word in each row. Find and circle two other words in that row with similar meanings. Use a dictionary if needed.

1. complete   finish   complain   end

2. instructions   errors   lessons   directions

3. discuss   talk   debate   disgust

4. example   ample   model   sample

5. respond   respect   answer   reply

6. define   explain   confuse   clarify

7. score   grade   mark   scare

B. Read each question. Choose the best answer.

1. Which one is a **passage**?   ❑ paragraph   ❑ chapter

2. How do you **describe**?   ❑ works   ❑ words

3. What can you **compare**?   ❑ berries   ❑ busy

Portfolio Page

Write a text message to a friend telling about a test you took. Use at least two vocabulary words from this lesson.

Name _____ Date _____

compare	complete	define	describe	discuss
example	instructions	passage	respond	score

A. **Some words have more than one meaning. Choose the word or phrase that gives the best meaning for the vocabulary word as it's used in each sentence.**

1. A narrow **passage** led from the
door to the room.   ❏ reading selection   ❏ hallway

2. Our soccer team had the highest **score**.   ❏ points   ❏ grade

3. Scott did the math **example** correctly.   ❏ model   ❏ problem

B. **Write a sentence to answer each question.**

1. What are two things you can **compare**? _____

_____

2. What is something you have to **complete**? _____

_____

3. What might you **discuss** with a friend? _____

_____

4. How do you **respond** to a compliment? _____

_____

5. How would you **describe** your hair? _____

_____

6. When you don't know a word, where do you find out how to **define** it? _____

_____

7. What **instructions** might you give a dog? _____

_____

180 Essential Vocabulary Words for 3rd Grade © 2009 by Linda Ward Beech, Scholastic Teaching Resources

Name _____ Date _____

Read the clues. Identify the correct vocabulary word and write it next to its clue. Then find and circle each word in the puzzle.

B	I	N	S	T	R	U	C	T	I	O	N	S
Y	K	D	T	U	E	A	O	X	C	L	V	C
D	I	S	C	U	S	S	M	G	N	Q	J	O
E	W	C	H	M	P	X	P	Z	P	S	P	R
S	F	R	V	B	O	T	L	K	I	C	A	E
C	D	E	F	I	N	E	E	D	A	G	S	W
R	U	O	L	P	D	J	T	R	V	C	S	F
I	C	O	M	P	A	R	E	Y	F	Q	A	J
B	X	H	S	B	T	Z	N	I	E	W	G	N
E	Q	A	R	D	E	X	A	M	P	L	E	O

Hint:
The words
can run
ACROSS
or
DOWN.

Clues

1. a set of directions   _____

2. talk about something   _____

3. tell what a word means   _____

4. identify how things are alike and different   _____

5. a model   _____

6. finish   _____

7. a grade on a test   _____

8. opposite of ask   _____

9. give details about something   _____

10. a short part from a written work   _____

CITIZENSHIP

Name _____ Date _____

adopt	contribute	cooperate	fulfill	goal
legal	opinion	rely	role	rule

✱ SOME WORDS ARE USED OFTEN WHEN TALKING ABOUT GOOD CITIZENSHIP.

When you **adopt** something, you approve or accept it.

If you **contribute** something, you give it.

By working together with others, you **cooperate**.

To **fulfill** something is to carry it out.

A **goal** is a purpose or aim.

Legal means "lawful."

An **opinion** is a belief.

If you depend on someone, you **rely** on that person.

A **role** is a position.

A **rule** is a guide for how to act.

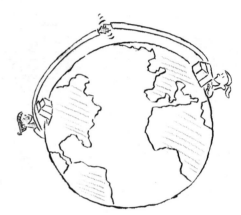

Use what you know. Write the best vocabulary word to complete each sentence.

1. Hal thinks caring for the environment is an important _____ .

2. Tammy agrees; she shares his _____ .

3. They both want to play a _____ in cleaning up a park.

4. They hope others will _____ to the cleanup, too.

5. If people _____ on getting the project done, the park will improve.

6. A better park will _____ Hal's dream.

7. Projects like this _____ on good citizens.

8. What main _____ would you suggest for using the play area?

9. The town will _____ some litter laws.

10. Then it will be _____ to fine people who litter.

180 Essential Vocabulary Words for 3rd Grade © 2009 by Linda Ward Beech, Scholastic Teaching Resources

Name _____ Date _____

adopt	contribute	cooperate	fulfill	goal
legal	opinion	rely	role	rule

A. Each of these words is found in one of the vocabulary words. Write the vocabulary word on the line.

1. tribute

_____

2. pin

_____

3. fill

_____

4. operate

_____

B. Read each question. Choose the best answer.

1. Which one is **legal**? ❏ law ❏ lawn

2. Which one is a **role**? ❏ relax ❏ part

3. Which do you **rely** on? ❏ friend ❏ enemy

4. Which one is a **goal**? ❏ game ❏ purpose

5. What can you **adopt**? ❏ mitten ❏ kitten

6. What do you do with a **rule**? ❏ ignore ❏ obey

Portfolio Page

Write a list of ways you can be a good citizen. Use at least two vocabulary words from this lesson.

CITIZENSHIP

Name _____ Date _____

adopt	contribute	cooperate	fulfill	goal
legal	opinion	rely	role	rule

A. Write a vocabulary word that is the opposite of each word below.

1. take

2. reject

_____

_____

3. illegal

4. mistrust

_____

_____

B. Write a sentence to answer each question.

1. What **role** would you like in a play? _____

_____

2. What is a **rule** you have in your classroom? _____

_____

3. What is your **opinion** about littering? _____

_____

4. What **goal** do you have in school? _____

_____

5. How will you **fulfill** your goal? _____

_____

6. Why should teammates **cooperate**? _____

_____

180 Essential Vocabulary Words for 3rd Grade © 2009 by Linda Ward Beech, Scholastic Teaching Resources

Name _____ Date _____

Read the first word in each row. Find and circle the word in each group that doesn't belong. Then, in order, write the words you circled to make a silly sentence.

1. contribute	donate	give	some
2. goal	aim	games	target
3. adopt	approve	accept	provide
4. legal	lengthy	lawful	permitted
5. role	position	pause	part
6. fulfill	amuse	meet	satisfy
7. opinion	opponent	belief	idea
8. cooperate	participate	help	order
9. rely	depend	enjoy	trust
10. rule	regulation	law	refreshment

Silly Sentence

_____ _____ _____ a

_____ _____ to _____ an

_____ and to _____ and _____

a _____ .

Name _____ Date _____

always	ancient	annual	brief	cycle
decade	final	never	schedule	sequence

✴ SOME WORDS ARE USED WHEN SPEAKING ABOUT TIME.

Always means "all the time."

Something that is **ancient** is very old.

An **annual** event happens once every year.

A **brief** time is a short time.

A series of events that happen over and over in the same order is a **cycle**.

A **decade** is ten years.

When something is **final**, it is at the end.

Never means "not ever."

A **schedule** is a list of events.

Sequence means "order."

Happy Birthday

Use what you know. Write the best vocabulary word to complete each sentence.

1. Each year, my grandparents' visit is an _____ event.

2. They have _____ missed a visit.

3. Their visit is part of the _____ of our year.

4. Grandfather is a _____ older than my grandmother.

5. His stories are lively and do not seem at all _____ .

6. I am _____ happy to see them both.

7. We plan a busy _____ of things to do and see.

8. Their week with us seems too _____ .

9. One year, they taught me a _____ of steps to a folk dance.

10. I feel sad when the _____ day of their visit arrives.

180 Essential Vocabulary Words for 3rd Grade © 2009 by Linda Ward Beech, Scholastic Teaching Resources

Name _____ Date _____

| always | ancient | annual | brief | cycle |
| decade | final | never | schedule | sequence |

A. Read the words at the base of each arc. Then write the best vocabulary word along the arc.

1.
program   timetable

2.
finished   last

3.
short   limited

4.
forever   unending

5.
order   succession

6.
old   aged

B. Read each question. Choose the best answer.

1. Which is in a **cycle**?   ❑ seasonings   ❑ seasons

2. What is in a **decade**?   ❑ years   ❑ weeks

3. Which one is **annual**?   ❑ checker   ❑ checkup

4. What **never** runs?   ❑ whale   ❑ wolf

Portfolio Page

Write a story about a favorite time in your life. Use at least two vocabulary words from this lesson.

180 Essential Vocabulary Words for 3rd Grade © 2009 by Linda Ward Beech, Scholastic Teaching Resources

TIME

Name _____ Date _____

| always | ancient | annual | brief | cycle |
| decade | final | never | schedule | sequence |

A. A prefix is added to the beginning of a word to change its meaning. The underlined words in the sentences below begin with prefixes. Read each sentence, then write what the word means. Use a dictionary if needed.

1. We will <u>recycle</u> our newspapers. _____

2. We will <u>reschedule</u> the event. _____

3. They will <u>debrief</u> the messenger. _____

B. For each number, read the three words. Use a colored pencil to shade the word in one of the bottom boxes that means the opposite of the word in top box.

1. | final |

| first | | funnel |

2. | never |

| ever | | always |

C. Write a sentence to answer each question.

1. What is something that is an **annual** event in your life?

_____

2. What is something you should do in **sequence**?

_____

3. What is something you should **always** do?

_____

4. What is something from **ancient** times you would like to learn about?

_____

5. In exactly one **decade**, what will the date be?

_____

60

180 Essential Vocabulary Words for 3rd Grade © 2009 by Linda Ward Beech, Scholastic Teaching Resources

Name _____ Date _____

Read the clues. Then, complete the puzzle using vocabulary words from this lesson.

Across

2. a program of events

4. very old

6. a period of ten years

7. the end

8. repeating events

9. a short amount of time

Down

1. forever

2. an order of events

3. happening every year

5. at no time

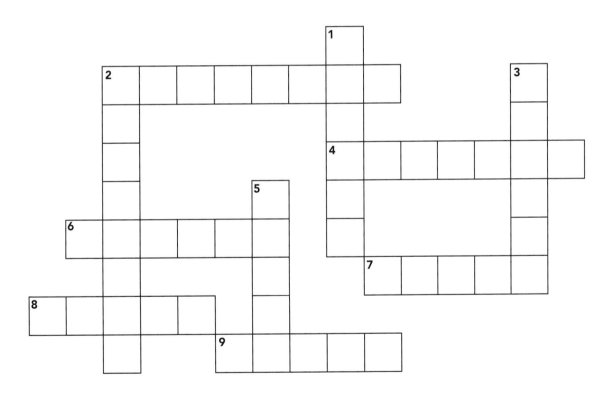

180 Essential Vocabulary Words for 3rd Grade © 2009 by Linda Ward Beech, Scholastic Teaching Resources

Name _____ Date _____

adjust	cause	explain	explore	fact
favorable	insist	outcome	reveal	summary

✱ SOME WORDS DESCRIBE WHAT HAPPENS IN A DISCUSSION.

Adjust means to change.

When you **cause** something, you make it happen.

Explain means to make something clear.

If you **explore** something, you investigate it.

A **fact** is something you can prove to be true.

Something that is **favorable** is pleasing.

When you **insist**, you take a strong stand.

An **outcome** is a result.

If you **reveal** something, you make it known.

A **summary** is a short retelling of a longer passage.

Use what you know. Write the best vocabulary word to complete each sentence.

1. A group often gets together to _____ a topic in a discussion.

2. Some people state a _____ that they know.

3. Others _____ their ideas well.

4. They _____ things you didn't know.

5. Some people _____ that they are right.

6. Can they _____ you to change your mind?

7. You might _____ your thinking after talking with the group.

8. You might have a more _____ opinion of some ideas than others.

9. A good _____ helps everyone review the discussion.

10. The _____ of a discussion can lead to action.

180 Essential Vocabulary Words for 3rd Grade © 2009 by Linda Ward Beech, Scholastic Teaching Resources

Name _____ Date _____

adjust	cause	explain	explore	fact
favorable	insist	outcome	reveal	summary

A. Write a vocabulary word that belongs with each group of words.

1. _____

show

disclose

open

2. _____

demand

compel

assert

3. _____

adapt

correct

change

4. _____

promising

encouraging

pleasing

5. _____

review

recital

retelling

6. _____

investigate

discover

search

B. Read each question. Choose the best answer.

1. Why would you **explain**? ❏ justify ❏ baffle

2. Which one is an **outcome**? ❏ question ❏ result

3. What is a **fact**? ❏ false ❏ true

4. Which one is a **cause**? ❏ reason ❏ consequence

Portfolio Page

Write a summary of a discussion you have had. Use at least two vocabulary words from this lesson.

DISCUSSION

Name _____ Date _____

adjust	cause	explain	explore	fact
favorable	insist	outcome	reveal	summary

A. These words have suffixes. A suffix is added to the end of a word to change its meaning. Underline the suffix in each word below. Then, write a sentence using the word. Use a dictionary if needed.

1. adjustment _____

2. insistence _____

3. factual _____

4. exploration _____

5. summarize _____

B. For each number, read the three words. Use a colored pencil to shade the word in one of the bottom boxes that means the opposite of the word in top box.

1. reveal
uncover | hide

2. outcome
input | result

3. favorable
unfavorable | pleasing

4. cause
affect | effect

5. explain
simplify | confuse

180 Essential Vocabulary Words for 3rd Grade © 2009 by Linda Ward Beech, Scholastic Teaching Resources

Name _____ Date _____

Play the New Word Game.

Read each clue, then write the word or word part from the lesson word. The first one is done for you.

Vocabulary Word	Clue	New Word or Word Part
1. favorable	Find a suffix.	*able*
2. insist	Find a family member.	_____
3. summary	Find the answer in addition.	_____
4. reveal	Find a kind of meat.	_____
5. explain	Find a landform.	_____
6. adjust	Find the opposite of *unfair*.	_____
7. outcome	Find two words.	_____
8. fact	Find a stage activity.	_____
9. cause	Find the opposite of *disuse*.	_____
10. explore	Find a mineral.	_____

Name _____ Date _____

arrange	attach	copy	inspect	operate
recover	require	restore	reverse	seek

✱ A VERB IS A WORD THAT SHOWS ACTION. THESE ACTION VERBS ARE USEFUL TO KNOW IN SCHOOL.

When you **arrange** things, you place them in a certain order.

Attach means to fasten.

If you **copy** something, you reproduce it.

If you **inspect** something, you examine it.

When things **operate**, they work.

Recover means to get back.

If you **require** something, you need it.

Restore means renew.

When you **reverse** something, you make it go in the opposite way.

If you **seek** something, you look for it.

Use what you know. Write the best vocabulary word to complete each sentence.

1. Darcy lost her work and tried to _____ it on the computer.

2. This report will _____ more work.

3. Tyler helped _____ the books in the library.

4. The teacher said she would _____ a note to our tests.

5. Never _____ someone else's work.

6. The twins will _____ information in the encyclopedia.

7. Betsy knows how to _____ the microscope.

8. If you _____ the numbers, you'll get the problem wrong.

9. After the team went wild, the coach tried to _____ order.

10. The health board will _____ the lunchroom.

180 Essential Vocabulary Words for 3rd Grade © 2009 by Linda Ward Beech, Scholastic Teaching Resources

VERBS

Name _____ Date _____

| arrange | attach | copy | inspect | operate |
| recover | require | restore | reverse | seek |

A. Read the word in the first column. Draw a line to match it with a word in the second column that has a similar meaning.

1. recover   **a.** search

2. operate   **b.** check

3. inspect   **c.** regain

4. seek   **d.** reproduce

5. copy   **e.** run

6. attach   **f.** revive

7. restore   **g.** bind

B. Read each question. Choose the best answer.

1. Which can you **reverse**?   ❐ autumn   ❐ auto

2. What can you **arrange**?   ❐ beads   ❐ bears

3. Which one do humans **require**? ❐ sleep   ❐ television

Portfolio Page

Write about a project you have worked on at school. Use at least two vocabulary words from this lesson.

Name _____ Date _____

arrange	**attach**	**copy**	**inspect**	**operate**
recover	**require**	**restore**	**reverse**	**seek**

A. A prefix is added to the beginning of a word to change its meaning. These words have the prefix *re-*. It means "again." Write a sentence using each word.

1. rearrange _____

2. reattach _____

B. Many words can be used as more than one part of speech. Write *noun* or *verb* for each vocabulary word.

1. Please **copy** the words from the board. _____

2. Please make a **copy** of this page. _____

3. Mara put the car in **reverse**. _____

4. He will **reverse** the order of assignments. _____

C. Read the words in each group. Write the vocabulary word that is related to each group.

1. _____   **2.** _____   **3.** _____

    inspection   operator   recovery

    inspector   operation   recoverable

4. _____   **5.** _____   **6.** _____

    requirement   restoration   seeker

    requisition   restorer   sought

180 Essential Vocabulary Words for 3rd Grade © 2009 by Linda Ward Beech, Scholastic Teaching Resources

Name _____ Date _____

Write questions and answers between two people. Use each of the vocabulary words at least once.

Questions   ## Answers

1.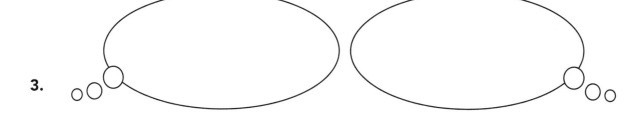

2.

3.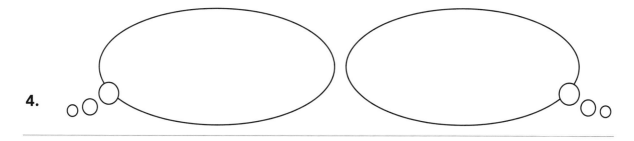

4.

5.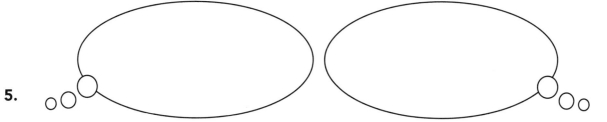

ADJECTIVES

Name _____ Date _____

available	enormous	extreme	major	medium
odd	rare	regular	sole	visible

✱ AN ADJECTIVE IS A WORD THAT DESCRIBES A NOUN. THESE ADJECTIVES ARE USEFUL TO KNOW IN SCHOOL.

Something that is **available** is ready for use.

Enormous means huge.

If something is **extreme**, it is at the highest degree.

Something that is **major** is very important.

Medium means in the middle position.

Odd means strange.

If something is **rare**, it is not often seen.

Regular means usual.

Sole means one and only.

If something is **visible**, it can be seen.

Use what you know. Write the best vocabulary word to complete each sentence.

1. Jim follows a _____ schedule at school.

2. The students read all the information that was _____ .

3. Is the video _____ from the back of the room?

4. To the small children in kindergarten, the school seemed _____ in size.

5. Maureen was the _____ student to raise her hand.

6. The _____ weather kept many students at home last week.

7. Graduation is a _____ event for most students.

8. Bill wrote his report about a _____ bird.

9. Nancy wasn't too tall; she was of _____ height.

70 **10.** Sometimes Carol's ideas seem _____ to her friends.

180 Essential Vocabulary Words for 3rd Grade © 2009 by Linda Ward Beech, Scholastic Teaching Resources

Name _____ Date _____

available	enormous	extreme	major	medium
odd	rare	regular	sole	visible

A. Underline the best ending for each sentence.

1. An **odd** request might cause you to _____ .
   a. respond quickly   **b.** shout loudly   **c.** think carefully

2. A **rare** book is likely to be _____ .
   a. valuable   **b.** ordinary   **c.** reasonable

3. Finding **available** help is important for an _____ .
   a. entrance   **b.** emergency   **c.** exercise

4. The **sole** person on a boat might get _____ .
   a. crowded   **b.** selfish   **c.** lonely

5. When you are driving, a **visible** landmark is _____ .
   a. hidden   **b.** helpful   **c.** dangerous

6. When a **major** holiday occurs, you may _____ .
   a. not have school   **b.** have more work   **c.** be late to school

B. Read the words at the base of each arc. Then write the best vocabulary word along the arc.

1.

immense   gigantic

2.

steady   normal

3.

middle   average

4.

excessive   most

Portfolio Page

Write an ad for something you might buy to use in school. Use at least two vocabulary words from this lesson.

ADJECTIVES

Name _____ Date _____

available	enormous	extreme	major	medium
odd	rare	regular	sole	visible

A. Some words have more than one meaning. Choose the word or phrase that gives the best meaning for the vocabulary word as it's used in each sentence.

1. Her dad was a **major** in the army.   ❑ officer   ❑ key

2. She had a hole in the **sole** of her shoe.   ❑ one   ❑ bottom

3. Nine is an **odd** number.   ❑ strange   ❑ not even

4. Radio is a **medium** for communication.   ❑ means   ❑ middle

5. Her teeth are straight and **regular**.   ❑ steady   ❑ even

6. Charlie likes his hamburger **rare**.   ❑ pink   ❑ scarce

B. A suffix is added to the end of a word to change its meaning. These words have the suffix *-ity*. It means "condition." Write a sentence using each word.

1. enormity _____

_____

2. extremity _____

_____

3. availability _____

_____

4. visibility _____

_____

180 Essential Vocabulary Words for 3rd Grade © 2009 by Linda Ward Beech, Scholastic Teaching Resources

ADJECTIVES

Name _____ Date _____

What's the Word?

Write the vocabulary words that fit the descriptions below.

1. Write a word that is the opposite of tiny.   _____

2. Write a word about the bottom of your shoe.   _____

3. Write a word that means peculiar.   _____

4. Write a word that a ghost would not use.   _____

5. Write a word that describes an "over-the-top" sport.   _____

6. Write a word that is between big and little.   _____

7. Write a word that describes a good heartbeat.   _____

8. Write a word that means uncommon.   _____

9. Write a word that is the opposite of minor.   _____

10. Write a word that goes with a "For Rent" sign.   _____

180 Essential Vocabulary Words for 3rd Grade © 2009 by Linda Ward Beech, Scholastic Teaching Resources

Name _____ Date _____

career	clue	code	earnings	expert
fee	item	notion	purpose	source

✱ A NOUN IS A WORD THAT NAMES A PERSON, PLACE, OR THING. THESE NOUNS ARE USEFUL TO KNOW IN SCHOOL.

A **career** is a profession.

A **clue** is a hint.

A **code** is a series of signals or symbols for sending secret messages.

Earnings are wages.

An **expert** is someone with great skill or knowledge.

A **fee** is a price.

An **item** is an article.

If you have a **notion**, you have an idea.

A **purpose** is a reason for doing something.

A **source** is where something comes from.

Use what you know. Write the best vocabulary word to complete each sentence.

1. Olive had a _____ about the story she would write.

2. Each week, Mrs. Rice put her _____ in the bank.

3. Ruth counted ten things on her dresser, one _____ at a time.

4. For fun, Jessie sent a message in _____ .

5. The _____ of this class is to improve reading skills.

6. Eric hoped to have a _____ in law.

7. The _____ of the puddle on the floor was a leak.

8. Mom thinks the plumber's _____ is very expensive.

9. Dr. Robb is an _____ in old maps.

10. The fingerprint is a _____ for the police.

180 Essential Vocabulary Words for 3rd Grade © 2009 by Linda Ward Beech, Scholastic Teaching Resources

Name _____ Date _____

career	clue	code	earnings	expert
fee	item	notion	purpose	source

A. Read the first word in each row. Find and circle the two other words in that row with similar meanings. Use a dictionary if needed.

1. notion	motion	belief	idea
2. source	origin	root	sour
3. career	work	careen	occupation
4. earnings	earrings	salary	wages
5. purpose	purple	intent	aim
6. clue	evidence	hint	clove

B. Read each question. Choose the best answer.

1. Which one is a **code**?   ❑ comb   ❑ secret

2. Which one is a **fee**?   ❑ charge   ❑ chart

3. What is an **expert**?   ❑ informed   ❑ reformed

4. Which one is an **item**?   ❑ oblong   ❑ object

Portfolio Page

Write a statement about your goals in school. Use at least two vocabulary words from this lesson.

Name _____ Date _____

career	clue	code	earnings	expert
fee	item	notion	purpose	source

A. Write a vocabulary word that is the opposite of each word below.

1. spendings   **2.** novice   **3.** ending

_____   _____   _____

B. Write a sentence to answer each question.

1. What **career** might you someday have? _____

_____

2. What is the most useful **item** in your desk drawer? _____

_____

3. When might you use a **code**? _____

_____

4. What is a **clue** a person leaves when he or she walks in mud? _____

_____

5. What **fee** would you charge for doing errands? _____

_____

6. What is the **purpose** of an umpire? _____

_____

7. What is your **notion** of a good adventure? _____

_____

180 Essential Vocabulary Words for 3rd Grade © 2009 by Linda Ward Beech, Scholastic Teaching Resources

Name _____ Date _____

Read each clue. Write the correct vocabulary word in the spaces below. Then, write the letters from the shaded boxes in order on the lines to find the mystery word.

1. the root of something ☐ ☐ ☐ ☐ ▨ ☐

2. reason or goal for doing something ☐ ☐ ☐ ☐ ▨ ☐ ☐

3. an article in a series ☐ ☐ ☐ ▨

4. a help to detectives ☐ ☐ ▨ ☐

5. an idea ▨ ☐ ☐ ☐ ☐ ☐

6. payment for work ☐ ☐ ☐ ☐ ▨ ☐ ☐ ☐

7. what a spy might use ▨ ☐ ☐ ☐

8. profession ☐ ▨ ☐ ☐ ☐ ☐

9. someone you call for the best advice ☐ ☐ ☐ ☐ ☐ ▨

10. a charge for services ☐ ☐ ▨

Mystery Word

The more words you know, the better you can

___ ___ ___ m ___ ___ ___ ___ ___ ___ ___ .

LESSON 1
Page 6: 1. subject 2. display 3. grade 4. partner 5. project
6. assign 7. team 8. elementary 9. primary 10. substitute
Page 7: A. 1. show, exhibit 2. replacement, alternate
3. activity, plan 4. crew, group 5. class, level **B.** 1. first
2. geography 3. homework 4. share 5. kindergarten **Page
8: A.** 1.–3. Sentences will vary. 1. substitut<u>ion</u> 2.
partner<u>ship</u> 3. assign<u>ment</u> **B.** 1. verb 2. noun 3. verb
4. noun 5. noun 6. verb **C.** 1. score 2. basic 3. person
4. simple **Page 9:** 1. elementary 2. display 3. substitute
4. subject 5. partner 6. team 7. primary 8. project
9. assign 10. grade; Mystery Word: educational

LESSON 2
Page 10: 1. fiction 2. setting 3. character 4. author
5. series 6. plot 7. period 8. paragraph 9. dialogue
10. detail **Page 11: A.** 1. setting 2. character 3. dialogue
4. plot 5. series 6. author **B.** 1. make-believe 2. end
3. information 4. sentence **Page 12: A.** 1.–4. Sentences
will vary. 1. author<u>ity</u> 2. fict<u>ional</u> 3. ser<u>ial</u> 4. character<u>istic</u>
B. 1. lot 2. time 3. place at a table 4. duty **C.** Sample
answers:1. autograph 2. diagonal **Page 13: Across:**
2. fiction 6. dialogue 7. paragraph 8. setting 9. period
Down: 1. plot 3. character 4. detail 5. author 8. series

LESSON 3
Page 14: 1. report 2. brainstorm 3. journal 4. outline
5. draft 6. audience 7. revise 8. edit 9. proofread
10. publish **Page 15: A.** 1. outline 2. audience 3. report
4. journal **B.** 1. first try 2. improve 3. end 4. share
C. 1. b 2. a **Page 16: A.** Answer order may vary.
1. brainstorm 2. outline 3. proofread **B.** 1. slight breeze
2. meeting **C.** 1.–5. Sentences will vary. 1. journal<u>ist</u>
2. revis<u>ion</u> 3. edit<u>or</u> 4. report<u>er</u> 5. publish<u>er</u> **Page 17:**
1. proofread 2. journal 3. edit 4. draft 5. audience
6. publish 7. outline 8. brainstorm 9. report 10. revise

LESSON 4
Page 18: 1. chapter 2. heading 3. topic 4. inform 5. main
6. text 7. caption 8. index 9. feature 10. quote **Page 19:**
A. 1. c 2. b 3. a 4. b 5. c **B.** 1. important 2. read it
3. column 4. insects **Page 20: A.** 1. pipe 2. branch
3. subtitles 4. forefinger **B.** 1. verb 2. noun 3. verb 4. noun
5. noun 6. verb **C.** 1.–3. Sentences will vary. 1. inform<u>ation</u>
2. text<u>ure</u> 3. top<u>ical</u> **Page 21:** 1. caption 2. main 3. index
4. topic 5. inform 6. chapter 7. text 8. quote 9. heading
10. feature

LESSON 5
Page 22: 1. graph 2. order 3. measure 4. chart 5. sum
6. plus 7. estimate 8. pattern 9. area 10. solve **Page 23:**
A. 1. problem 2. addition 3. guess 4. organize 5. change
B. 1.–5. Sentences will vary but should include the
following vocabulary words: 1. measure 2. area 3. pattern.
4. sum. 5. order **Page 24: A.** 1. summarize 2. field
3. steps 4. request 5. model **B.** 1. not solved 2. unknown
or unmapped **C.** 1. estimate 2. graph 3. plus

Page 25: 1. some 2. markets 3. carry 4. orange 5. lace
6. plain 7. socks 8. enormous 9. plums 10. grapes; Silly
Sentence: Some markets carry orange lace, plain socks,
enormous plums, and grapes.

LESSON 6
Page 26: 1. population 2. disaster 3. leisure 4. culture
5. job 6. tradition 7. trend 8. transport 9. event 10. export
Page 27: A. 1. happening, occasion 2. work, task 3. carry,
move 4. spare, free 5. accident, wreck 6. fad, direction
B. 1. exit 2. repeated 3. people 4. beliefs **Page 28:**
A. 1. job, leisure 2. event, trend 3. disaster, population
4. tradition, culture 5. export, transport **B:** 1. export,
transport 2. population, tradition 3. trendy, eventful,
leisurely **Page 29: Across:** 1. event 3. trend 5. leisure
7. culture 9. transport 10. population **Down:** 2. export
4. disaster 6. tradition 8. job

LESSON 7
Page 30: 1. globe 2. overseas 3. region 4. address
5. key 6. symbol 7. resource 8. label 9. locate 10. route
Page 31: A. 1. symbol 2. locate 3. globe 4. key 5. region
B. 1. country 2. place 3. information 4. road 5. useful
Page 32: A. 1. speak to 2. turn lock 3. skills 4. sphere
or ball 5. foreign **B.** 1. verb 2. noun 3. verb 4. noun
C. 1. region 2. symbol 3. locate **Page 33:** 1. locate
2. symbol 3. route 4. label 5. resource 6. globe 7. overseas
8. region 9. key 10. address

LESSON 8
Page 34: 1. energy 2. environment 3. habitat 4. survive
5. migrate 6. absorb 7. launch 8. conservation 9. adapt
10. technology **Page 35: A.** 1. e 2. c 3. f 4. a 5. b 6. g 7. h
8. d **B.** 1. technology 2. conservation **Page 36: A.** 1.–5.
Sentences will vary. 1. surviv<u>al</u> 2. migra<u>tion</u> 3. energ<u>ize</u>
4. habita<u>tion</u> 5. adapt<u>ation</u> **B.** 1. c 2. b 3. c 4. b 5. a
Page 37: Across: 4. conservation 5. absorb 6. launch
8. energy 9. migrate 10. adapt **Down:** 1. survive
2. technology 3. environment 7. habitat

LESSON 9
Page 38: 1. inquire 2. demonstrate 3. identify 4. affect
5. discover 6. category 7. forecast 8. preserve 9. review
10. conclusion **Page 39: A.** 1. answer 2. destroy 3. lose
4. preview **B.** 1. affect 2. category 3. conclusion
4. forecast 5. identify 6. demonstrate **Page 40: A.** 1.–3.
Sentences will vary. 1. affec<u>tion</u> 2. discover<u>y</u> 3. forecast<u>er</u>
B. 1. ending 2. report 3. show opinion **C.** 1. identify
2. preserve 3. category 4. inquire **Page 41:** 1. discover
2. identify 3. review 4. preserve 5. conclusion
6. demonstrate 7. inquire 8. category 9. affect 10. forecast;
Mystery Word: investigate

LESSON 10
Page 42: 1. study 2. list 3. plan 4. notes 5. predict 6. link
7. recall 8. file 9. test 10. research **Page 43: A.** 1. connect
2. organize 3. past 4. lesson 5. words 6. remembering

7. check **B.** 1.–3. Sentences will vary. **Page 44: A.** 1. line 2. lean 3. sounds 4. take back 5. room **B.** 1. verb 2. noun 3. noun 4. verb 5. verb 6. noun **C.** 1.–2. Sentences will vary. 1. research<u>er</u> 2. predict<u>ion</u> **Page 45:** 1. storage 2. join 3. inventory 4. record 5. program 6. forecast 7. remember 8. search 9. learn 10. exam

Lesson 11

Page 46: 1. draw 2. illustrate 3. form 4. pose 5. create 6. trace 7. design 8. visual 9. exhibit 10. style **Page 47: A.** 1. formless 2. destroy 3. hide 4. erase **B.** 1. sketch 2. sign 3. model 4. fashion 5. composition 6. artist **Page 48: A.** 1.–5. Sentences will vary. 1. creat<u>ion</u> 2. design<u>er</u> 3. illustrat<u>ion</u> 4. exhibit<u>ion</u> 5. styl<u>ist</u> 6. visual<u>ly</u> **B.** 1.–3. Sentences will vary. **C.** pose **Page 49:** 1. trace 2. form 3. create 4. design 5. visual 6. draw 7. illustrate 8. pose 9. exhibit 10. style

Lesson 12

Page 50: 1. discuss 2. instructions 3. respond 4. example 5. complete 6. passage 7. compare 8. define 9. describe 10. score **Page 51: A.** 1. finish, end 2. lessons, directions 3. talk, debate 4. model, sample 5. answer, reply 6. explain, clarify 7. grade, mark **B.** 1. paragraph 2. words 3. berries **Page 52: A.** 1. hallway 2. points 3. problem **B.** 1.–7. Sentences will vary. **Page 53:** 1. instructions 2. discuss 3. define 4. compare 5. example 6. complete 7. score 8. respond 9. describe 10. passage

Lesson 13

Page 54: 1. goal 2. opinion 3. role 4. contribute 5. cooperate 6. fulfill 7. rely 8. rule 9. adopt 10. legal **Page 55: A.** 1. contribute 2. opinion 3. fulfill 4. cooperate **B.** 1. law 2. part 3. friend 4. purpose 5. kitten 6. obey **Page 56: A.** 1. contribute 2. adopt 3. legal 4. rely **B.** 1.–6. Sentences will vary. **Page 57:** 1. some 2. games 3. provide 4. lengthy 5. pause 6. amuse 7. opponent 8. order 9. enjoy 10. refreshment; Silly Sentence: Some games provide a lengthy pause to amuse an opponent and to order and enjoy a refreshment.

Lesson 14

Page 58: 1. annual 2. never 3. cycle 4. decade 5. ancient 6. always 7. schedule 8. brief 9. sequence 10. final **Page 59: A.** 1. schedule 2. final 3. brief 4. always 5. sequence 6. ancient **B.** 1. seasons 2. years 3. checkup 4. whale **Page 60: A.** 1. reuse 2. schedule again 3. question for information **B.** 1. first 2. always **C.** 1.–5. Sentences will vary. **Page 61: Across:** 2. schedule 4. ancient 6. decade 7. final 8. cycle 9. brief **Down:** 1. always 2. sequence 3. annual 5. never

Lesson 15

Page 62: 1. explore 2. fact 3. explain 4. reveal 5. insist 6. cause 7. adjust 8. favorable 9. summary 10. outcome **Page 63: A.** 1. reveal 2. insist 3. adjust 4. favorable 5. summary 6. explore **B.** 1. define 2. result 3. true 4. reason **Page 64: A.** 1.–5. Sentences will vary. 1. adjust<u>ment</u> 2. insist<u>ence</u> 3. factual 4. explor<u>ation</u> 6. summar<u>ize</u> **B.** 1. hide 2. input 3. unfavorable 4. effect 5. confuse **Page 65:** 1. able 2. sis 3. sum 4. veal 5. plain 6. just 7. out, come 8. act 9. use 10. ore

Lesson 16

Page 66: 1. recover 2. require 3. arrange 4. attach 5. copy 6. seek 7. operate 8. reverse 9. restore 10. inspect **Page 67: A.** 1. c 2. e 3. b 4. a 5. d 6. g 7. f **B.** 1. auto 2. beads 3. sleep **Page 68: A.** 1.–2. Sentences will vary. **B.** 1. verb 2. noun 3. noun 4. verb **C.** 1. inspect 2. operate 3. recover 4. require 5. restore 6. seek **Page 69:** Questions and answers will vary.

Lesson 17

Page 70: 1. regular 2. available 3. visible 4. enormous 5. sole 6. extreme 7. major 8. rare 9. medium 10. odd **Page 71: A.** 1. c 2. a 3. b 4. c 5. b 6. a **B.** 1. enormous 2. regular 3. medium 4. extreme **Page 72: A.** 1. officer 2. bottom 3. not even 4. means 5. even 6. pink **B.** 1.–4. Sentences will vary. **Page 73:** 1. enormous 2. sole 3. odd 4. visible 5. extreme 6. medium 7. regular 8. rare 9. major 10. available

Lesson 18

Page 74: 1. notion 2. earnings 3. item 4. code 5. purpose 6. career 7. source 8. fee 9. expert 10. clue **Page 75: A.** 1. belief, idea 2. origin, root 3. work, occupation 4. salary, wages 5. intent, aim 6. evidence, hint **B.** 1. secret 2. charge 3. informed 4. object **Page 76: A.** 1. earnings 2. expert 3. source **B.** 1.–7. Sentences will vary. **Page 77:** 1. source 2. purpose 3. item 4. clue 5. notion 6. earnings 7. code 8. career 9. expert 10. fee; Mystery Word: communicate